MILES PRESS

Indiana University South Bend Department of English

YOU
ARE
STILL
ALIVE

42 Miles Press
Editor, David Dodd Lee
ISBN 978-1-7328511-0-8 (pbk. alk. paper)

42 Miles Press, Department of English, Indiana University South Bend
1700 Mishawaka Avenue, South Bend, IN 46615

http://42miles.wordpress.com

Art Direction: Nick Kuder, Design: Ashton Butler, Production: Paul Sizer
The Design Center, Frostic School Of Art, Western Michigan University.
Printing: McNaughton & Gunn, Inc.

YOU ARE STILL ALIVE

POEMS BY WILLIAM STOBB

CONTENTS

III. Ark

A MESSAGE FROM YOUR MODE

Some of the distant shadowy figures
responsible for your passage here
continue to be like you, i.e., alive,

awkwardly wired with conflicting motivations
such as empathy, rage, desire, fear
and a devastating need to be known.

This chorus / hoard endorses transportation
as a mountain is transported
which is not to say slowly, but with evident poise.

Smoke if you like. Part of you burns.
                    Should you feel
discomfort or uncertainty, pause:

consider the tranquil practice
of the Bushido at Yomei-gaku.

They studied virtue and dueled for honor
harboring live goldfish in their mouths.

I. ATMOSPHERE

To stay alive, you have to hold out against equilibrium, maintain imbalance, bank against entropy. When the Earth came alive it began constructing its own membrane for the general purpose of editing the sun... the first thin atmosphere.

—Lewis Thomas, from *The Lives of a Cell*

Feel the tension in the air we're breathing
and breathe heavy
and breathe largely

—Doomtree, from "Bangarang"

ENTROPIC

At the bench along the marsh by the munitions bunker,
boarded-up nature center & Catholic cemetery
there's noise in the air—traffic & birds—
call it pollution or call it singing.

In an afternoon lecture on anti-anti-
pornography feminism, I learned one re-
enlightenment protocol affirms even the brutal
orgies of de Sade over the endless
expansion of particles to void.

Here's a tipped-over heron sculpture
on an overgrown patio where the band once played
featuring the local singer who appeared on TV.
We danced with a sense of our own imminent arrival
but when the marsh ice vanishes and the winter count
of dead fish surfaces, we'll smell
the relevant processes in action.

Carp don't leave monuments, as far as I know.
And although the President's planning
to wall us in I think it's comforting to remember
that geology shrugs off all insults in time.

In the houses around the park, kids hunker
in basements—it's hard to blame them—
connecting across continents
to save a world that seems to matter
from the persistent dead, back again,
all dumb & ugly & famished.

INTERVAL

It shouldn't be rare, this ability
to sit quietly in history, a statue
of St. Francis tucked among woody
trunks of old Lilac—a kind of
dopey looking saint my sister gave me
after her husband quit the ministry
left her with the girls
and became an architect over in Ames.

On today's date, a comedian
and a salesperson of air time
are divorcing down my block.
Their teenage daughter fronts a punk band
so collapse immediately becomes chorus.
A looming cloud formation
threatens biking plans, as distant nail guns
fasten down roofs. Prayer,
an idea, circles like birds
as a breeze sets the chime.
Two translucent insects hover
above irregular stalks of grass
and two families down the alley
have lost sons in the wars.

Dogen Marty tells me
"if you're not afraid of death
you're afraid of fear."
I struggle most with the anger
that spills out of me like yesterday
when I yelled at my children for simple carelessness.
Marty's trying to help me
regain my composure
but I think I pretend, mainly,
to understand my motives.

I've been reading this morning
in a plastic chair that will outlive words.
I want to learn something
from the stories Betsy writes,
in which the emotional life
inflected by the brightness of wit
puts its arm around the intellect
and leads it back inside.

PUBLIC SERVICE ANNOUNCEMENT

Stifled by negativity?
Consumed by futile thinking?
Before committing any felonies,
breathe, count to ten. Remember:
everyone shares a point of origin
in the big bang, best conceptualized
by our local remnant ember
the sun—
take a moment now
to frame that burning orb
at the center of your mind: a giant orange
of intensely gravitational electro-nuclear fire—
how hot is that bastard? you might wonder
& I checked: twenty-seven
million degrees at the core
poised to someday go supernova
& swallow our whole system
in fire before sucking back (with a tiny pop?)
into a pinhole spiked through
the fabric of this big old sweater we
call the universe—
you may recall being
outside at night with friends by a fire
listening to music & also talking
about families & dream jobs & favorite
ballplayers & problem behaviors you're trying to
rein in because you want to get it
right in this life & you're grateful
for these friendships: real
good things you can feel & just then
the fire snaps

& you watch a bright spark
shoot up & hover in the thermal pressure
& you say *it's like the sun* & imagine it
fueling every single human thing
that ever occurred in history, spinning & floating
—it's beautiful, right? with some pine trees
& every epic love lynching war masterpiece
gift theft disease attack slightest
gesture of kindness like her glance &
hand coming to rest on your shoulder
all provided by the spark
until it blinks out & zip, everything
stops & there's only a density of
absence retaining zero
evidence of histories personal
slights political failures just
no life okay
     thank you
we can be done now it's
impossible anyway to imagine the nothing
ahead the massive fragility of our speck in this
exploding second I'm sorry
this was only an interruption
like an advertisement
for the original heat & light
that sponsored all life.

POEM WITH THE VIRGIN MARY

January's figures don't add up:
degrees too high, flocks too low
riding southerlies out of Iowa, where
one town has a big red cherry for a water tower
and lo the Virgin appears in a pattern of birds
entering weather's mistake.

It's like this now: sugary blood-tears trickle
down ceramic cheeks as a store clerk peels
burrito foil to find her in cheese and cilantro.
In the convent parking lot, a morning frost
etch-a-sketches her countenance on a Nissan.
Last week, a quarterback's stat line was all numerology
to Mary wide open in the end zone, while
the Christian gift shop downtown featured
bobble-head virgins blessed by the Pope.

Me? I've been trying to flood an ice rink in my yard.
My hundred billion covalent bonds
struggle against this winter's fizzle
to spin a transition around their appointed points
of immeasurable gravity and trans-
substantiate themselves from liquid into a surface
frozen solid enough for a peewee to practice his wrister.

I spray hopeless slush and drift and dream:
the Virgin Mary, her hands like a hockey official's
clasped behind her back skating
deliberate figure eights in the sky.

WHAT IS HAPPENING

As the era of blue radar concludes
I Scotch tape a storm spiral
to the place on my mirror
where my face would appear.
It will be hard to explain
believing in something larger
than the brands—I wanted
to think originally
but only used adhesives—"it's wanting
what you have" sang the singer
who loved the biker
who swapped his tainted blood each week.
Iridescent flies
I think of as tiny
(though the bottom of that well
never plinks) vector against human
children currently
climbing our splintery
fence to play house in our decaying fort
with dangerous rope swing over
polluted sandbox guarded by broken
saint statue forever
amen that is until someone ahem
paints his head orange
making him gaudy and soon to be
transported to another realm.

What is happening
seems mainly about to happen—
a fade into a possible other
sandbox with rusty truck
and many buried Batmen.
A thermo-dynamic feeling: deep in in-
and external space

centrifugal forces grind
coastlines and dopamine receptors
smother former pleasures
in the era's terminal wreckage.
One anxious lover
hatches a desperation scheme
to stave off depression
by enhancing sex with ice cream
which seems like a great idea
at the time.

TIME

I liked illustrations
of time's expansiveness

like if you lined up
dollar bills

each representing
one millennium

you could wrap them around the moon
a hundred million times

and there you'd be

at the end of the line

trying to jam the current epoch
into the Coke machine

outside Walgreen's.

SYNCHRONIZED SWIMMING

Except walking
where an old Cadillac U-turns
mirrored shades make me
I think for a cop

over-heated and over
-exposed I am
dizzy and I duck
into the avenue gallery

where a grizzled burner's
playing electric guitars
made from toasters and coat buttons
pictures hanging all of water

may be ironic but if I
plug my ears I do still hear
ocean inside this
synchronized swimming routine

twirl of wallet and *voila!*
two Hendrix postcards
mine for a dollar and endurance
of cashier eye-rolling

surprise I carry off
a passable plié
we're alive after all
and afloat in this day

pause against the glass
door between me and
a tangle of terriers in the street
where is my car where

do I go I don't know I do
make the door chime the air
too hot and visibly
pregnant one pit bull

locks my eyes I recognize
skinny trees buckle and release
exhausted by the brutal
choreography of the sun

TWO CITIZENS

The morning my elected representative trades
nuke threats with North Korea, I
drink less coffee—in a nuclear winter scenario
coffee might not be available.
When I was a kid, my mom had surgery
and had to quit cold turkey.
She survived only with headaches and nausea
for a month solid and I'm so dependent
crippled by withdrawal
how will I manage to scour the wastelands
for any sign of life?
So it's two cups only
and all afternoon I stare at sparks
reeling around a red
maple on 10th avenue
like sparrows around a
scorched head. My mind slips up
into the jet stream and blazes
a contrail across the map of the planet until
I'm hovering over the streets of Pyongyang where
my enemies dressed all in gray and brown
frown and shake their fists at the sky.
Beaten dogs whimper.
Ball-gagged women writhe in the gutter.
Infants twitch at the buzz of their shock collars.
One citizen jaywalks and
officers with approved haircuts immediately
incinerate him with flamethrowers.
Right? No? Someone
stands at a sink in despair?
Hears sparrow song in his maple and
imagining great suffering
denies himself a cup?

DURING A PANIC ATTACK, I WATCH A BUDDHIST DOCUMENTARY

and breathe and breathe and *become*
the English captions on the English language film
                              I explain
the Serpent Bridge's decay
the gray-haired god vanishes I say
in the *truck* of a tree   not sure why
monks are making clay
-mation stop-action movies
for English-on-English translation
but I announce that they're webcasting
the monastery bell
                              I narrate
over the silent meal
and when the visiting dignitary steals
a pastry from the chef's rolling tray
I laugh five times in brackets
and imagine myself healed

personality   resumes

depressing thought experiments
lost action figures embedded
in a grassy hillside dissolve in ivy
more slowly than species
                              when future
sentient beetles excavate the site
will they find a religion
in our superhero costumes?

we want to capture a planetary feeling
says the Venerable Master of Animations
Earth will miss its failing clay bee

spiraling into the forest
remembering nothing
of attraction   broken
                              and why now
do I remember the captain
of the volleyball team
guiding my fingers   pressing
                              breath
accelerating into pleasure

                    a feeling like outside

          river and sky

     expanding   I'm afraid

          I wanted this
                    living like a child
          wants every form of sugar

GREEN APPLE INN

Arriving at this farmhouse bed and breakfast
where the organic fair houses guests this year
I've been listening to the news update
troubling with rape and baseball
so I am baffled and a little beside myself
when the woman who lives in the north rooms
greets me with the scripted story:
black cherry lumbered from family acreage
bricks won from river clay and one
green apple allegedly
plucked from the orchard beyond the corn.

What a Brinks job this life can be.

The spring pond spawns streams
of high school seniors posing for pictures.
The original barn's hewn beams
bend to brace the arc of wedding dance rental.
When she sees me notice the sticky spot
where the label's been peeled from the apple skin
her eyes beg me not to mention it.
I'm grateful for the attic room with its view
of the flooded quarry, shimmering
in late sun. I sit at a wooden desk all afternoon
imagining the generations
who've leapt from the granite overhang
to plunge into cool insistent truth.

PRETEND VAN LEEUWENHOEK

Antonie Van Leeuwenhoek,
"Father of microscopy," 1632-1723

Walking home through the stadium neighborhood
ambient sounds feel orchestrated:
bright pip of trumpet
clang of cowbell
and a voice announcing field events over a PA.

All week the town's been filling with buses
carrying runners to the capital
for the seasonal tournament.
I like to pretend
Van Leeuwenhoek peers

down through a pinhole in the sky
observing the spike in ice cream sales
and losses of virginity.

He reports increased volatility
to the Royal Society
before a light lunch and posing
for the next Vermeer.

Meanwhile, on the slide
I'm alive and aware
of names and times threaded through
drapery of cloud. Runners to marks
and the gun, the crowd

crescendos to a roar, so loud I'm sure
Antonie will have to close the aperture
all apologies to the master of light.

CAPITOL STREET PULSE

I've been here an hour and haven't seen his pitch work. "Donate for
    Street Pulse?" in a major arpeggio and then "have a nice day"
    back down on the black keys.
My friend's friend's dead uncle, Woody Guthrie, might be patron
    saint of the scene: three acoustic guitarists variously perched, girl
    in a sequined tracksuit spinning on roller skates.
On the capitol lawn, someone's barking loudly into the rotunda,
    though I think he only wants to hear the sound, not advocate for
    any cause.
Yesterday, police used bullhorn threats to clear a protest against
    police violence. The governor says he'll print the names of
    anyone involved, but it's okay:
practically everyone's on the list. Lately in my bones I can feel tiny
    protestors slowing the flow of oxygenated blood—this tissue
    warrants no supply! this tissue warrants no supply!
Not enough little bubbles are clearing customs, and my eyelids,
    murderous most recently of spinach, have begun to flutter
    and twitch. Beautiful
day for the Catholics picketing the nearby hospital against abortion,
    while recent internet searching shows nineteen open cases of
    child abuse against local clergy.
I almost succeed in not thinking, "it's like they want to keep the
    fetuses alive so the priests can rape them later," but not quite. I
    guess this is the everyday horror of thought.
At the next table, three engineering students use their big brains to
    sketch the circuitry of sunglasses that will project holographic
    movie clips in the air around our heads.
We'll buy scenes like ringtones and illuminate ourselves with
    Hollywood. I'd buy the guy holding his baby in the rain shouting
    Good luck exploring the infinite abyss!
Street Pulse features reports and opinions on private Mars colonies
    with an illustration of caravans on a dusty red road exchanging
    cargo pants for onions. Like anyone, I'm hoping

we'll get behind peace and love before we colonize the solar system,
   but I'm still noticing people's bodies more than their sense of
   responsible citizenship.
Maybe it's easier to believe in the enduring virtues of the glute
   rounding up from the hamstring than the Jeffersonian column in
   the floodlight at dusk.
On cue a jogger passes with PINK on her butt, and here's a painting
   of a Dodo in a tilting frame. *Google Conquers Death* is the title
   on the next table. Somewhere in Texas
a mad billionaire schemes to start it all up again on a brand new
   planet, but I'm just busing my cup and leaving *Street Pulse*
   behind. On my way to the bus stop, I wonder
if a distant descendant will someday hover over this rubble, detect
   and uncover the digital time capsule hologram we've left to run
   on solar in the ruined rotunda.
*Good luck exploring — // * Good luck.*

OF BIRTH AND PANAMA

Pairs of what you wish and what you know
Fledged cardinal chirping in the ivy

The unbreakable commitment broken
The world born anew without words like anew no

Pears sliced without toast crumbs on no
Counter, fractal screen saver slipped

In the harness, horses painted in
Underwater caves and leather

Boys crying and shrugging: a history
Borne through canals of birth and Panama

The Van Halen song with car sex lyrics
On the hospice piano, a mascot

With an ascot! for your sexual history
Flour in five-pound bags shotgunned

On Independence Day, scour the island
To find the banana bread lady

Up the treacherous mountain highway
New beaks evolve to surf soundtrack

Everyone blink six million times
To sleep perchance to peep

THE DREAM OF PERFECT PANTS

After Dean Young

This morning I dreamed of the perfect pants.
They looked like regular pants, sometimes, but
they were *responsive*, like a mood ring, so
they became whatever I needed. Yes.
I knew it was a dream because I worked
in a regular office and I went out at night
to swanky clubs with attractive friends
who complimented me on my pants.
You know how dreams are like reality
on uppers—these pants kept revealing their
properties in scenarios that morphed
and overlapped. I was dancing with Tanya
and my pants under the disco ball kind of
glistened and then my pockets filled
with birds flew me up to a low Earth orbit
where I triggered special magnets in my pockets
and solved the global problem of space debris.
I spoke to the assembled sales force: "too
long we've been shackled by ordinary
things. It's time to set loose our dreams." People
laughed, I guess because it *was* a dream, but
my pants became angry and vaporized
the sales force, and strangely, the image of
that moment became the catalogue ad
for Power Pants, which was branding I had
not approved. In response to my subsequent
frustration my pants became massaging
pants, and in response to my subsequent
arousal my pants became intimate
pants. And in response to my subsequent
confusion my pants gave counseling.

As I became perfect, my pants became
messianic, attracting disciples.
I felt at that point the pants
should become robes, but no dice
—in this dream pants were pants—
so I sang karaoke and the disciples danced
to that Motown classic "Gimme Those Pants"
and when I woke and found my wardrobe
unimproved, I realized again
how little I had to lose.

A MOMENT FOR AUTHENTIC SHINE

This is the greatest moment of your life,
said the voice both familiar and distant, like a childhood
friend become spokesperson for a cleaning product—
which caused the many hats to turn in many directions
and one robed arm to extend.
And what after all had been passing?
The sounds birds made often seemed more cogent
than the swirl of argument, a cyclone in a sandbox.
So much management we ought to have degrees
was a type of joke made at outmoded parties.
Still with shades and declarations
echoes of heroic solos translated out of urgent decades
while almost unnoticed, pensive tunes accumulate in the mix
like thunder clouds on these warmer days. Regardless,
names come unpinned, stars die, a closetful of semi-
recognizable jackets and hats bespeaks
the by-gone, and yet the baffling rekindling of romance
may justify the maintenance of a hairstyle.
A certain heart medication—no, I was afraid to say
a certain heart, beating in the chest of a certain girl.
To say heart in that trite way, and girl when by now she's fifty,
and real when the elapsing of all things into void
has been made abundantly clear. But I knew her
and she seemed real, and at thirty still childlike—
a trait adorable in women, rather of concern in men
say the conservatives but look who's ogling
the ballplayers around the pool table.
Any slogan invites rebuttal, and a spin into personal views
often doubles futile conversation. One might live
consuming nothing but packaged goods and still
in that moment of late afternoon crash—
over-heated, nauseated by sexual memory,
blinded by sun, buffeted by wind—unfairly rely
on that prideful sense of authenticity

so prized in our time that it could be said to float,

invisible of course, above a century's worth of steaming wrecks—

cloud of elemental and reckless

identity unwarranted, silver-lined illusion of nobility—

until geographies choke in the torrent,

shrines assembled from knick-knacks manufactured

by prisoner children dissolve

and in our true magical forest

blossoms wreathed by small creatures

that worked in tandem with our spirits become,

as we become, atmosphere.

II. FUTURE CAVE PAINTINGS

Behold! human beings living in an underground den, which has a mouth open towards the light....

You have shown me a strange image, and they are strange prisoners.

Like ourselves.

—Plato, from *The Republic*

MEANING

There were stars in the sky and stones on the ground, and the feeling was
          correspondence. Slow and steady.
There was mud and blood and if you ground up leaves or flowers, thinned it with
          piss, smeared it on a boulder,
you could be the dream cave painter.

                                           *

On the wall above the toilet in the men's bathroom at the J.T. Bar and Basque
          Restaurant in Minden, Nevada:
framed photograph of an image carved by a shepherd into the bark of an aspen
          tree, circa 1870: human male puts his exaggerated penis inside a
          sheep.

So many questions. Was that carver your average shepherd? Is "perv" a more
          complicated designation
when it's 1870 and it's just you and those sheep, day after week after month after
          year, with those eyes, those real vaginas?

Or maybe the carver never even had sex with sheep. Maybe the carver thought
          that doing it with sheep was a *hilarious* idea, and he carved it to be funny,
          his laughter echoing on the mountainside the only human sound for a
          hundred miles.

                                             *

I don't think it was supposed to be a gerund, honestly. Meaning. It was supposed
          to remain transitive. A person could *mean* something specific, like...
          scribble it down and hand it to you: *your fly is down, call 911*, etc.,
but you couldn't just stand there *being* significant in that way that makes me
          wonder about your lips.

*

We hoped meaning would arrive. We figured we'd be happy when it came, like
        the one friend who makes your whole social circle work, when that friend
        is late for the barbecue and you're all staring at your phones.

It could be like a dream, at times—a distant possibility. Other times you could
        notice a distinct lack of it, like being out of syrup or not feeling loved.

People pointed to motion picture technology. We're always driving at night
        (psychologically) past a drive-in movie as the stars lean in to kiss.
We know their anticipatory sighing can be heard on a low FM frequency, but too
        late: we're already past and looking out the passenger window at those
        other stars, also glamorous, just farther away.

*

Doing yard work I would reflexively reach to the peg board for the Masterforce
        Titanium Lopper.
Ninety-nine times I would go a-prunin', and never consider the tool. One time,
        though—the way it says China, the design of the lever—the back, the
        yoke, the yardage—I thought of
falling in love with that lopper. I didn't fall in love with that lopper, but I
        imagined making out with it
and while I did laugh inside, I also shuddered—think of those vicious blades all
        over your body.
Finally, I decided there must be some evolutionary advantage of being capable of
        such a misconception.

*

My major obsession was with finding a deep cave, where I would spelunk into a
        recessed cavern and there paint pictures of iPads, Camrys, and cases of
        frozen pizza, so the future might know our speed and light.

In real life, I was killing mice because the apocalypse movies du jour featured
        houses overrun with vermin
feeding themselves on the rotting corpses of former middle-class families who'd
        succumbed to whichever plague the movie was selling.
All I could do, I felt, was mistakenly-preemptively treat the symptom.

Story logic was a major factor. If everyone got what they deserved according to
        the insinuated code
then you'd feel good, like you'd just eaten a satisfying snack, and maybe that was
        it—click: the experience of meaning.

But you didn't have to push very hard—well, who wrote the code? who taught the
        coder?—and you'd be off in the spiral-y, cartoon void of outer space
        where all our thought-waves wiggle away in static.

THE FUTURE

Conscience was tossing pebbles at my window in the night, so I took to recording
        stories of people who'd survived catastrophes.
It was a way beyond serving omelets to better the world within the boundaries of
        my skill set. And I did sleep better for a while.

Then the stories began seeming ordinary—everyone's house was hit by a tornado—
        and as everything became debris around everyone—as the boat capsized
        and everyone hit the frozen water, as the support chopper crashed and
        everyone emerged pointing guns at everyone—everyone believed his
        or her life was simultaneously precious and pretty much over.

Talking with me was a kind of non-experience, from a time they'd given up on.
        The future? Sure. I guess.
You can find them on cassette in the oral history archives.

*

With fortune cookies, "the future" arrives in bed. "By watching out for your
        fellow man, you watch out for yourself (in bed)."
A significant percentage of second dates that begin with Chinese food end with
        "think with your mind, work with your hands (in bed)." That was a
        good one.
Which is also what God said to his buddies after his week-long bender at Void
        Nineteen. "That was a good one (in bed)."

*

There were apostles. And there were certain postulates. And a small hawk
        resting on a long stalk of marsh grass.

When you've admitted that everything is real. Whatever else it might be.

Basho tried to stop creating images, you know—asleep on horseback, the sunken
        moon—and when he couldn't stop, he felt weak, and never forgave
        himself.

*

For a while the future was planning to contract back to whatever pinpoint aurora
        into a new crowd crush or even back through and inside-out into a spooky
        negative of us.
Smarties tried every way of explaining, and finally arrived at the balloon-pulled-
        through-a-peephole idea, which both made sense and made clowns seem
        even more powerfully creepy.
Soon enough we learned that not even a giant master clown could match the
        power of entropy, which will go forever pulling until the balloon's a thin
        disc of rubber, basically—a slap shot toward what goal?

*

By living according to core values, we can carry on daily tasks in the face of
        insignificance. Conserve fossil fuels. Avoid the plastic cycle.

Too much looking around can lead to paralysis due to inevitable recognitions of
        unfathomable vastness, which cast consciousness as infinitesimal quirk.
Keep to your routine. In the future, smaller, more focused organisms may survive
        slightly longer.

DOOM

To describe the timpani part at the beginning of Strauss's Zarathustra, you could
    say doom doom doom doom doom doom doom doom, and then you'd
    probably sing up with the trumpet part, as if a twisted brass tube could
    escape fate.

                                    *

Doom is one of the early first person shooter games that people got addicted to.
    You were "Doomguy" and you shot your way through thousands of goat-
    faced demons from Mars.
In Russia, I saw men sit at public terminals for days at a time, playing *Doom*,
    urinating into their empty Mountain Dew bottles.
I also saw alcoholic men writhing in the gutter, and a uniformed soldier open a
    beer bottle with his arm stubs.

                                    *

One conversation reached the conclusion that everyone's depressed—how could
    you sail on the burning funeral ship of the species, your own body,
    watching the landscape of extinction pass on the receding shore, and be
    essentially well-adjusted?
"Look at us," said D.: "everything we're wearing, drinking, eating, is totally
    fucked,"
and even though we were on a bright patio at a sushi place in Chicago, I felt a
    foreboding sense, as in a horror movie, that a spear would be thrust from
    the ground up through my body and out my mouth, leaving me gagging
    blood while everyone ran, screaming.
It was a secondary sense, though, which allowed me to continue my lunch,
    because obviously stuff like that rarely happens.

*

Awesomely, after about one minute of finger wiggling, I am able to start
        Kubrick's *2001* on my laptop and I can tell you that the Zarathustra
        trumpets come before the timpani.
And now the crescent moon. And now the approaching sun.

And even for the dawn of humanity that music is almost too much.

*

You may recall the super-villain, Victor Von Doom. He forged a metal mask to
        cover a small scar on his cheek.
Unfortunately, he donned the mask while it was still smokin' hot, and burned the
        shit out of his face. That's when he started calling himself Doctor Doom,
        but maybe he should've called himself Doctor Just Wait Five Minutes.

*

The mind is always running on multiple tracks, I think, but then I recognize that
        that very thought is swiped from audio production software. Thinking
        doesn't work that way, probably.

Most times thinking feels perfectly normal.

Thinking can even be boring, even oppressive. One positive thing about death might be
        the end of having to think.

*

Now the people in ape costumes are going "scram, scram" at each other, and then
        the cheetah is poised over its kill, sunrise gleaming in its eye, on the day
        that that domino thing arrives from outer space
and the ape is able to imagine using a large bone to bludgeon another ape and then
        immediately does so and becomes human.

*

The oldest use of Doom I could find was the title for the law book of King Alfred
        the Great, circa 900.
This book is so awesome that the Ten Commandments are the *preface*—that
        would be my blurb for it.
Back then, "doom" meant something like "law" or "judgment." "Doom very
        evenly!" King Alfred liked to say. "Do not doom one doom to the rich and
        another to the poor!"
And it sounds like Alfred was pretty strict. "If he belie himself and be slain, let
        him doom uncompensated," and I get a very *doomy* image from that:
a big red-bearded Viking lying in the mud, bleeding out from an axe wound,
        blinking his last blinks knowing that no one has prayed for him in the way
        you need to be prayed for if you're going to heaven.

And the camera pans up into the sky and into our solar system and our galaxy and
        our universe, but the heavy string music continues over top
because my capacity for imagining stuff is afflicted with the sappy conventions of
        my time

(as if Viking heaven required beseeching prayer—I'm pretty sure Vikings just
        attacked and took over their heaven, which wasn't even called heaven—it
        was called V-something—Valhalla. Yes.)

which I cling to as if they had a merit I would someday defend to an art critic god.

"Those were great accomplishments," I'd say.

"Sweeping strings. Chest-swell and stifled sob. You have to concede the skill and dedication to craft."

But I guess for a god it's pretty relative.

III. ARK

*I have wanted and still want to depart this life with specimens of people,
flora and fauna, to lodge them all in my heart, as in an ark.*

—Danilo Kis, from *Hourglass*

Everything is actual, everything is real.

—Lawrence Weschler, from *Mr. Wilson's Cabinet of Wonder*

WUNDERKAMMER

Rocks came alive when McGaferty applied
                 a tiny magnet to the blood.
He holds a rigor mortised gerbil in the photo.
His wife stands balanced on a gnome.

Moist planty oxygen in the brightly lit terrarium.
Two ducks splash down in a fountain
turned orange by pennies' oxidation.

Powder blue snowmen guard the observatory
where Marty found the pecs of Perseus
during *Dark Side of the Moon*.

In the *kabinet*, the private life seems
elegant in a Danish style:
sleek blinds and a herring figurine.   Sturdy
      (actually it's decomposing)   teak.

Something like a towel rod might never become
a great nation's symbol
                 but transcendent
    even of independence   hockey boys
    sing *O Canada* in the shower.

At closing time a line of drivers curbside:
              one in a flat cap
holds a sign with a single word: *STAR*.

SAM SAYS EVERYTHING

's weird if you stare at it and I'm staring
at the travel graph of the Voyager craft—
the one that sailed past all our planets

taking the pictures I've framed of Jupiter's
big red eye, ice geysers on Enceladus
and the spooky blue of Neptune.

A while back I emailed the childhood friend
who became a past life regressionist.
She told me life began on a distant moon

which made life seem kind of middling, to me—
side-shelved and orbiting around
whatever the real real thing might be.

One time late at night on a golf course
we kissed and she said it wasn't right.
I still wonder specifically why.

She replied to say *a good way to go insane
is to constantly ask what's wrong with yourself
and expect someone to answer*.

She also said *I thought you died*
and all week I wondered if it might be true.
I've heard reality's a function

of expectation, so my problem
stems from my prospect: I seem to be
clinging to the idea of a satellite

way out in the frozen night
beeping news from the motherland.
Like my own aging mother

sending clippings about potato blight,
poisonous spiders, New
Zealand's musical theater scene,

and the township's announcement
that the golf course has been sold
to an investment group out of Manitoba.

Just tell me: was it the mosquitos?
Were my lips dry or ineffective in some way?

Beep... Beep...

        I was just saying hello.

Beep... Beep...

        but I guess I would like to know...

after Sam Lipsyte

OTHER ODYSSEY

The explosion that everything is
quickly zooms back to the struck match.

Our Voyager says *distant stranger,*
think of me sometimes but doesn't know
that the Vogels, Sheldon and Anna,
already own *Cattle of the Sun God.*
Odysseus becomes a cat name, Argos a tame
quartet playing *Take Five* in the lobby.

World's worthy adversary, your great
grandchildren assemble your travels again,
suspect you're bullshitting
when you describe the magnetic
fields of Ganymede and start talking
like you think you can navigate.

ALBUM

He has some old ideas. He has some rubbish ideas. He is fussy. He hates
   our couch.

Life has passed him by. His truck has collectible value. He goes to farm
   auctions and bids low just to be involved.

Life has passed him by. His pictures of early flying machines make cool
   décor but he thinks he's still an engineer.

He wants to see the children, but he doesn't like the children. He likes
   the show about ice truckers.

When he was seven, he smashed his father's hand with an awl. When he
   was seventy he found PornHub.

He probably loaned out his weed-whacker but he says drug addicts
   broke into his shed.

For love, he went to Canada. She featured advanced badminton skills
   and not-having-a-husband.

Of the ice truckers, he likes the independent woman best, then the retired
   farmer, then the honest young bartender.

In fairness, he fixed many items, remained married, and drug addicts did
   break into a nearby barn.

He thinks every idea should be free. He says he'd have murdered the
   committee if they'd sent him back to China, but he never puts away
   his Forbidden City scrapbook.

He left the farm. His brother got the farm. He worked to help farmers
   but his program was cut. What will happen to farms and farmers
   and farming?

He watches young white people in foreplay and traditional coitus. His desires are anticipated by his browser.

Tonight he is going out for meat loaf. His empty dog kennel howls at the moon.

Tonight he is going out for meat loaf. His Pontiac passenger seat hovers empty in the moonlight.

SURFACE TENSION

January 23: minus 11: auburn
moth clung momentarily to the window screen.
It must've been alive.
Then an arctic downdraft slapped it to the snow crust
and it skidded past the barren elm
into neighboring corn stubble.

I've been helping a large man to toilet and bathe.
My second chance, he jokes
but he won't be seen by anyone.
He watches game shows in bed.
Joker... Joker...
An airplane crossing over
heads even further north.
The phone rings once and stops.
Mistakes are being made all the time.

~

The sun comes out and the wind settles down
after noon while he's sleeping.
I bundle up and walk the county road.
Two cows in a farm yard.
Their breath clouds around them where
someone's put down hay.
One bird sings in the river gorge.
Its chest a tiny cavern.
Its porous bones threaded into actual air.

CAPITAL OF BEARS

Early thaw so a bear sleepwalks
down one slick sandstone trail

knocks a few cans
in the neighborhood past the Empire Builder
winds up in the empty
cemetery acre past notable locals and Franciscan Sisters.

Don't know what it's digging for.
Squirrel nuts maybe crazed with
hunger maybe maybe

in bear world there's secret sugar
angled in by freight after freight

rippling the tracks: a mile away
my daughter's bookcase rattles & I think great,
poltergeist. The 2 a.m. wrong numbers
for strippers just finally slowed down.

Availability of my women? Sorry, limited
by the fact one nurses the other
in a rocking chair we're leasing.

When she was born
I wanted a word for future fear

& hope like bears biting each other's faces.
Like a tracker I follow
the debris trail & rapidly appearing
cell phone photos of

Our Local Bear
looking like a neutral bystander
at the stations of the cross

paw-tapping the vaulted doors of the private tombs
finally ripping into the any-old-someday grave

along the avenue by the Kum & Go.
Another city's sprung up
under the pavement.
I guess it's the capital of bears:

Honey holes un-glow in that un-lit world.
Wilders fire projectiles at an idea like salmon

& a crack opens, pulls a flint into
an explosion someone could worship.

CONTACT. IT'S HEARTBREAKING

how close it can seem
in a landscape touched by fire
like at the geyser
along the crater rim where
Steve lost Cookie
and we heard the coyotes
alarmingly near
but then John found Cookie
sleeping at the edge
of the fire circle: phew!
so we went ahead and swam illegally
in the amazing mineral pool
and Cami said this
is how life began
hot bacteria surfacing
and we laughed
because hot bacteria's a funny
nickname for Cami and we
thought it would never
end. We became
best friends in pools
just cool enough not to boil us.
Being a geologist
Frank broke everything
down to its functional units—
which became a band name:
The F.U. for short—
but I just wanted to love those moments
that seemed to land—
striking, we say,
because knowledge is covered in welts

Tectonics and fission,
eon, serotonin, asteroid, alcoholism.
Generation in retreat
across basins and ranges
from the fault line boundary
of the next Atlantis,
reverse pioneers
remain fibrous and
pulmonary to smoke in the very
same caves where ancestors
composed with a rock
against a rock
a spiral.

DIG

Salt ships out of dead sea.
Star cluster burned on clay sarcophagus.
Queen buried with bracelet of five
thousand gerbil teeth found in five
thousand years. Yes, Judy. Yes.

In case a later researcher can somehow hear our air
I'm saying Judy, Judy in sexually religious tones.
The film will be narrated by James Earl Jones.

Petrified Ostrich eggs in dry lakebed.
Evidence of cat worship anticipated, confirmed.
Off to the side Judy's daughter builds a tomb
for the future giant worms who might

pause while depositing eggs in its shade
to consider the architect's emotional state.

SORRY, I CAN'T DESIGN YOUR FUTURISTIC BUG CREATURE

"The problem is I'm already making
a sci-fi trilogy about a cruel beetle race
originally based on the Eastern Eye
Click Beetle but with the sheen
characteristic of the Neon Weevil.
I designed the neural ganglia center
in the middle of their pointy little faces—
a totally fake thing I invented
that caused gag reflexes in focus groups
triggering the influx of backing funds that subsequently
earned me the very contract that's buying these vodka crans.
Which, yes. Awesome. Thank you. Unfortunately,
they've got me in a non-compete.
So also, no. Bummer. Sorry. But hey:
can I just tell you that it's true?
The future seems predictable in the first two
—human depravity and global collapse.
Bugs emerge from festering pustules
less evil than opportunistic. Block by block
the major cities are devoured, while plagues
o'erwhelm the countryside until
somewhere in Saskatchewan the final human
gets sucked down by the glistening hive.
Yada yada yada. But in the new one,
when the millipede kingdom emerges
based on the wisdom of telepathically cooperative industry
and the bitchin' karate possible
for creatures with a thousand legs,
the numbers shoot through the freaking roof.
These beetles don't just succeed
in inheriting the Earth. Eventually
they harness cosmic forces and sail
into the great beyond. Then the question

is just *so real*: will they handle their godlike power
better than we handled ours?
Whoa. I know. Really, though
all I do is make their faces look gross.
One beetle makes interesting squeaky
sounds and the caption reads [beetle love song].
Then these two iridescent 'pedes
push their faces together in a kiss and it's like
eight mucus-y strands of feces
licking at an old brown tomato.
And that's my thing. That's where my craft
makes an impact on this town, nome sayin'?
After that it pretty much just ends.
Two lovers head out to sea on a leaf.
Probably tragic lover suicide, which raises
the question does anyone want to live
in a future where beetles commit suicide?
But there's a chance they'll survive and maybe
mate and mate and mate and mate and
rapidly evolve into an amphibious species that could rise
in yet another sequel like huge lobsters
on the shores of the millipede capital
and wreak havoc against the heartless
kingdom that shunned them.
So it's an ending. But is it also
a beginning? Whoa. I know."

POEM FOR THE VERY BEGINNING

I hadn't remembered the black screen, the first minute of *2001*. It sounds like
          strings are warming up, and they should get limber.
I would've watched cathode ray tubes warm up. I would've listened to the pulses
          of children in monkey suits.
To be honest, I'd been starving for transcendent anything. I went to those caves.
          I lay down on the highway. I'm renewing my vows in a week.
I don't care about the obelisk—I get prime delivery on those. The weapon bone,
          the hallway spinning. I do like her hat.
I did name something Hal but it was a personal device. I don't care about the
          embryo in the black hole space bubble and I'd sacrifice Dave even for
          the one second bright orange silent desert sunset right after the eclipse
          and symphonic power chord. Which is awesome.
But it's literally one second.

The best part is the beginning, where there's some radiance in the black like
          there might be a small fire just to the left of the world, and the strings
          begin to prepare.

THE CONCLUSIVE GESTURE BECOMES VISIBLE

oh no not that old saw
I think about so many endings
sci-fi classics I stayed up watching
discarded lives unlucky
survivors howling in the wastelands
and the brutal musical score
that today is sickly sweet on the tongue
of my co-worker who once died
in a car crash but Padre Pio
sent her back from the light
so she could short-shrift colleagues
through dismal middle years think

of all the extras dead in initial
explosions plagues infestations attacks
who might've traded oblivion
for any old cave-scrabbling indignity
maybe become the surviving
bloodline that one holy thing
preserved and holy equals
innocent in the sci-fi classics
all evidence to the contrary see

steaming wreck on mountain highway
ice crashing down from ruined trees
over steep embankment onto ticking hot
shattered hulk of the Volvo
instead of the Padre's robed arms
waving *back! back!*
and then awakening
in the hospital to begin

the long complaint:
my side boy only wants one thing
the service here is terrible
they don't pay me enough to explain—
better than this litany of worldly
disappointments maybe silence

in a picturesque mountain setting
is the best possible conclusion
or the second best
because you have to admit Charleton Heston
on the beach on his knees
in front of the ruined statue of liberty
is pretty tough to beat

FUN

I found the Kennedys today
down at Riverside Park: Jack in a v-neck
the color called Seafoam in the crew catalog
throwing a football with the lanky junior
eleven and all legs, juking, beaming
at his living father and laughing
when the President yelled
"cold in here? start the fire!"
which made no sense on such a balmy day.
Every word seems so precious
since they've all gone away.
Strange to find them here, where the wide river
crotches open to expose the mill
with its decaying factory, long conveyer
and reposed cone of quartzite.
I don't mean to emphasize *crotch*
in a crass way. Industrial parks
have positive aesthetic qualities
when seen with some perspective.
Smokestacks provide scale and chart
the sweep of human history
and I don't mind imagining the distant
giants of industry who've built our era:
all the Richards, Teds and Daryls
on such a day piloting their yachts
while Camelot's football wobbles
into the shadow of our large Hiawatha statue:
a Zimmerhakl, Anthony, 1962.
History describes it as a tumultuous era,
the sixties, when justice and peace
might've broken free of slogans
and become a kind of reality.

But I think Bugs Bunny was the greater
influence on Zimmerhakl, whose huge pastel Chief
seems most poised to step back into a TV
that might be loaded on an ACME truck
and driven off a cliff. Aaaa. Poof.
Our Hiawatha, arms crossed with a peace pipe,
high above the paddle wheeler and friendship
garden, makes history fun, as Jack would've
wanted for everyone—life-long
fitness and satisfaction in a land beyond
skirmish or treaty, fuel or distribution,
a stretch of bronze in setting sun.

FREEDOM

You had to be alone to experience freedom. Or with one person you loved.
        Beyond that, obligations set in and the condition slipped the county line.

People frequently criticized the association of freedom with automotive travel, but
        wouldn't Thomas Jefferson, Harriet Tubman, Lewis and Clark and Black
        Elk love a Cadillac ride across the inter-mountain West, spitting seeds,
        listening to some distant ball game on AM radio, watching geology pass in
        a time-lapse they never imagined?

There was one part about justice, one part about guns, one about money, sex, and
        land.

Horses and trucks. Chickens and ducks. I witnessed a Mallard's mourning once,
        on a golf course.
Its life mate lay dead in the rough, and the bereaved bird flew and returned, over
        and over, as if to coax its lover back to life with the prospect of one last
        spin around the bunker.
Finally, it rested next to her. It was sobbing in human terms. The realization of its
        loss and sudden alone-ness was affecting the visible behavior of the duck.

By imagining all creatures' representational systems, the precious glimmer of
        freedom can make you giggle and cry in an earnest way if wonder is still
        available to you.

One time, I drove all night with a woman I'd previously made out with. I took a
        gamble and played music I liked, though I thought she'd find it weird,
but she just laid her head in my lap and I rested my arm along her body, and I
        drove while she slept.

IDENTITY

Beyond all the cards
and paperwork (identity's a concept
surrounded by red tape
or police tape or maybe
caution tape *Cuidado! Piso mojado!*)
there was something else.
Something... deeper.

Like a Matryoshka doll
you might go in and in
until you're living in a nice development
on the outskirts of a rhizome
working nine to five
at a quark factory
deep in the heart of Will Bulka's kneecap
and that might be it:
your core identity.
You wake up and immediately
consume problematic commodities.

Still, if this inner force
justifies your actions
you remain untouchable.
You're you, and the world will have to
deal with that. And of course
it will.

DEAD AND ALIVE

I'd been peeing off that side deck forever
—peering moon obscured by overgrown flora
so it felt like a private experience
though the splashing might've been
recognizable to a neighbor or passerby—
until one night a bright beam of light
descended from the sky.

I was on the phone providing basic information
to a salesperson agreeing to replace
my stereo speakers. I'd just
unzipped and released
when the stream suddenly glistened
and the ivy exploded in pitchy white
and to my horror I saw
a spider the size of my face
rising on luminous filaments
from the festering underworld
where my landlord Nona Marigold
planted roses with no sense of irony
before moving to Hawaii
to harvest coffee beans as therapy
for neck and soul as the world began
to close up shop at the end of that era.

I for one had been wondering
if I might already be dead for the most part
when that unreal light invaded the moment.
Instinctively whimpering at cilia
gleaming on the spider's ropy thighs
I recalled a Raid can under the sink.
With surprising acuity I pinched my flow
nimbly zipped, scampered, snatched and
blasted that arachnid with aerosol poison

never compromising the new speaker conversation.
I understood that such an adept killer
could only qualify as *alive*.

Phone pinned to shoulder I stood
holding the cylinder in a circle of light originating
at a helicopter that eventually
moved along, scanning the neighborhood's
shadowy entryways, startling cats
from low-lying shrubbery.
The next morning I learned a security officer
had been murdered with a hatchet
just a few blocks away
so while that thick spider
floated in a death cloud
a man bled out and a suspect fled
under a blanket in the back of a Saturn.

Earthquakes began in the foothills
opening shafts into the mantle.
A sinkhole swallowed a duplex.
The whole world seemed to quiver.
On its way to the football stadium
the officer's funeral procession
funneled past my side deck where I
no longer exposed my tender parts to air.
Speakers arrived and a singer sang
everything makes sense in ten
thousand year increments. Captured
at a Utah Denny's, the suspect admitted
he'd always feared his nature.
Found guilty, his sentence was life.

POEM WITH NAMES CARVED INTO IT

In the display case at the outlaw gallery
a rack of bullets with names carved into them:
Finn, Barker, Howard, Stack.
I said to my daughter
I could never do that.
What, she said, shoot someone?
No, I said, carve tiny letters into compressed explosives.
So you'd shoot someone, she said. Great.
How could you carve that small? I continued
as we wandered into the adjacent café.
You'd almost need a tiny
person with a large power tool—large
relative to the little dude, I mean. Dad.
And you'd fasten the bullet
down with relatively large clamps
for stability. Dad. Then you'd erect a scaffold
around the bullet, climb up there and
crank up that power tool and carve
with delicate precision
the name of your enemy
without puncturing the bullet's casing....
Finally she punched me in the shoulder
and pointed to the TV in the corner.
A reporter in a coastal town
captured amazing live footage
of people slogging through the street
water up to their knees
staggering and raising themselves
against gale force winds
to fire rounds from handguns
at the wall cloud of a tropical
storm carrying a name to landfall.

SPEED WOBBLES

Looking out at the Rockies through a
Plexiglass oval, I reconsider the Star Child theory:
dropped by spaceship on a remote clifftop,
adolescent alien sacrifices itself
in a mountain stream, its blood seeding the planet
with the building blocks of humanity.
Spaceship goes *zip ---→ bing!*
and we're not supposed to wonder
who invented the inventor. Sure,
diagram hemoglobin 'til the cows come home
but whose cows are they?
Whose home really? My parents
had a system of blood-dumping chalices
sprung by a torture device and
strung through millennia on catchy phrases
like a Mouse Trap game.
Local nuns pray constantly in order
to keep a line open to the big whatever-it-is.
Meanwhile John goes silent
for ten rotations each orbit, and that
would make sense if sense wasn't a word.
To plug into the flow, my boy
puts on headphones, rolls out on his longboard.
One day he hits the slightest
bump in the pavement & a wave of increasing
amplitude ripples & bucks through his deck:
The Speed Wobbles. Control
blinks away and he's launched at the curb,
a pure arc of electricity pinwheeling
against the sky. It's an origin story:
wired to crash and survive, his mythology begins
a little scraped and tangled but alive
in the Petersons' arbor vitae.

YELLOW, RABBITS

Biking in to write about a bright
yellow color for a psychic's color catalog
I think how life breaks
my children's hearts in various ways each day.
Someone doesn't call doesn't like
someone back someone feels like the weird kid
who just hangs out with his dad.

All red ideas. I pedal on.

Remember the huge beanbag chair
back in that corner by the art books?
I might finally sit in that baby today
although it's brown—I wish
it were yellow. I just want to find out
who painted that stick-figure Don Quixote
black and white except the yellow sun
on Don horse and windmill.
Something about that hunched
delusional hero and the forever-white
at the edge of combustion.

Dwarf star. I grew up

in a yellow house. My parents drove
a yellow Malibu Classic wagon.
I once slept ten hours in the backseat
woke up in a Kansas
City parking ramp and when I
stood it was a hundred degrees.
The world passed very quickly
through every yellow
on its way to a white beyond consciousness.

Heat signature. I want the pain

to be worth it when they think someday
about yellow I want my children to know
Rothko brushed it over a thin layer
of rabbit collagen glue
to make us feel we might fall in and up
and if they think about the rabbits
everywhere continually born and dying
mainly violently they'll understand
all yellow burns through
into what wide outside.

NOCTURNE

A few days alone in a rented loft.
In the kitchen, hand-pressed rosemary vinegar,
coarse bread, arugula, two cherry tomatoes.
On the bookshelf, pan flute, yoga poses.
In one painting, twin expressions
of harpooner and breeching whale—
some kind of rage to be more
than alive. In another, panicked eyes
of mule deer fleeing a fire hung ironically
below the empty plastic circle
where the smoke detector should be.

I know one writer used his manuscript
for rolling paper, converted pages
of hard-won phrases into smoke
until markets reopened after war.
I've seen the vacant block
where a careless spark engulfed a gallery.
No one will again see Van Gogh
as he saw himself walking
a sunny field in overalls, pain
only dull in his ears, vertigo only
a slight wobble for one good afternoon.

If fire rolls through in the night
and my world becomes the new world's fuel,
not alarmed, I'll simply climb
my own staircase with a lullaby
like those Austrian children escaping the Reich.
Good night highline trumpeter
backer of the Supremes.
Good night cloud island over desert valley.
Good night tennis executive
whose pubic hairs I laminated.

Designer of clam-based
textile branding concepts, beer.
Good night beer. I'm not ashamed of us.

My loves downstream, I turn forever
toward you, grateful for our time.
As I see you, know that I accept you exactly.

And to the darkness
beyond the leaky window air-conditioning unit
with bobble-head Buddha and beach
volleyball photo, please help me
into silence. This life is all I can remember
and I'm afraid to let it go.

NOTES

The title *You Are Still Alive* comes from a concept by visual artist Landon Sheely. One of his YASA pieces hangs at The Root Note café in downtown La Crosse, Wisconsin, and I saw it there just as I was grappling with the title of this collection (which, at first, was *Synchronized Swimming*). When I saw the piece, it immediately connected in my mind as a central concept, a central-feeling present in this collection. I approached Landon about using the phrase as this book's title, and he was very gracious about it. I'm insanely grateful for his permission, and for all he does for the arts and social justice activism in La Crosse and beyond. His remarkable works are available in many forms and varieties, for viewing and for purchase, at landonsheely.com.

"Entropic"—Kathryn Parker, "Communal Sexuality: Mutual Pleasure in Sade's *La Philosophie*." Nicholas David & the Feelin' and Reed Grimm. 45th President of the United States of America, Donald Trump, promised to build a wall between the United States and Mexico to prevent illegal immigration.

"Interval"—Betsy Wheeler, *Loud Dreaming in a Quiet Room*. After Dogen Zenji, a 13th century Japanese Zen poet and philosopher. "Dogen" isn't actually an honorific. It's just a name. So calling oneself "Dogen Marty" is like calling oneself "Daryl Marty" or "Steve Marty."

"Public Service Announcement"—November 8, 2016.

"Two Citizens"—As 45th President of the United States of America, Donald Trump warned that North Korea would suffer "total decimation" if President Kim Jong-Un did not negotiate to end the nation's nuclear weapons program. After a meeting in 2018, however, the relationship between the two leaders became less volatile. President Trump expressed his admiration for President Kim Jong-Un, who is treated with reverence by his citizens, under threat of imprisonment or execution. "He speaks and his people sit up at attention," said President Trump. "I want my people to do the same."

"During a Panic Attack, I Watch a Buddhist Documentary"—Beijing Longquan Monastery, Venerable Master Xuecheng. Thanks to Professor Haixia Lan of the University of Wisconsin-La Crosse.

"Green Apple Inn"—Kickapoo County Fair, La Farge, Wisconsin, home of Organic Valley corporation.

"Pretend Van Leeuwenhoek"—Van Leeuwenhoek posed for Vermeer's paintings, *The Geographer* and *The Astronomer.*

"Capitol Street Pulse"—Madison, Wisconsin, protest against the 2015 shooting of Tony Robinson, an unarmed, 19-year-old African American Male, by a police officer. The officer was not criminally charged in the case, though the family won a $3.35 million dollar settlement to its civil suit. La Crosse, Wisconsin anti-abortion protests at Mayo Health Center, 2014. SpaceX Mars Colony—SpaceX plans to launch in 2022 a preliminary mission to "confirm water resources, identify hazards, and put in place initial power, mining, and life support infrastructure," in support of larger missions to begin in 2024 which would establish bases and take the first steps toward building civilization on the planet. Zach Braff, *Garden State.*

"Of Birth and Panama"—"Reach down, between my legs, ease the seat back." David Lee Roth. Aunt Sandy's Banana Bread, Maui, Ke'anae Peninsula, Road to Hana, as described by my beloved wife and best friend, Kari Houser, as well as Andrew McCarthy, star of *Weekend at Bernie's.*

"The Dream of Perfect Pants"—after Dean Young, "If Thou Dislik'st What Thou First Light'st On"

> I had come to the house, in a cave of trees,
> I had dreamed of the perfect gray pants,
> I have a life that did not become...

"A Moment for Authentic Shine"—Atmosphere, "The List": "it stretches for as far as the eye can see / it's reality—fuck it, it's everything but me."

"The Future"—for David Krump, Will Bulka, Doran Wright, Ben Humphrey, & Nick Plunkey. You inspire me and your friendships keep me alive.

"Doom"—Victor Von Doom is the arch-nemesis of Marvel Comics' Fantastic Four. The Law Code of King Alfred, circa 893 CE, is also called Doom Book, and stipulates that "if a man kills another man by letting a tree fall on him, the tree shall be given to the kinsmen of the slain."

"Wunderkammer"—Walker Arts Center, "Midnight Party" exhibition; Gary Hume, "Back of a Snowman."

"Sam Says Everything"—Sam Lipsyte's "The Dungeon Master." For Bridget Pilloud, see www.petsaretalking.com.

"Other Odyssey"—after Romare Bearden's collages at Chazen Art Museum, Madison, Wisconsin.

"Capital of Bears"—treed black bear fatally shot in Myrick Park, La Crosse, Wisconsin: though the bear was not posing an immediate threat to life or property, the DNR warden was not carrying a tranquilizer gun, and it might've taken an hour or longer for a tranquilizer to be obtained. "These are unpredictable wild animals," said the La Crosse police officer who made the decision to kill the bear.

"Contact. It's Heartbreaking"—Cottonwood grove in Black Rock Desert, near Fly Geyser, north of Gerlach, Nevada.

"Dig"—drafted at a lecture by Archaeologist Katherine Grillo on communal cemeteries of the Turkana Basin in northwestern Kenya. Also inspired by Michael Heizer's *City*, a massive Nevada land sculpture under construction since 1972, currently scheduled to open through the DIA Foundation in 2020.

"Sorry, I Can't Design Your Futuristic Bug Creature"—*Starship Troopers* TriStar Pictures, Touchstone Pictures, Big Bug Pictures (1997). Paul Verhoeven, dir.

"Poem for the Very Beginning"—for *2001: A Space Odyssey*, Stanley Kubrick originally wanted the actors playing early man to appear nude in full-body make-up, but this concept earned an X-rating from the MPAA, so at the last minute, Kubrick settled for children in monkey costumes, along with two actual baby chimpanzees.

"Fun"— For decades, Ho-Chunk Nation leaders have objected to this statue's kitschy style, and its implication that Native American history exists strictly in the past. As of 2019, the Zimmerhakl family has agreed to move the statue to private land if $50,000 can be raised to support its transportation. For a full history of the statue, and a discussion of Native American cultural representations in and around La Crosse, Wisconsin, see "My Wisconsin," a video production by historian Ariel Beaujot.

"Identity"—For Ken Nordine, 1920-2019, American author and voice artist, beat generation figurehead, and creator of "Word Jazz." See www.wordjazz.com.

"Dead and Alive"—1998 killing of Sgt. George Sullivan, University of Nevada, Reno, by Siaosi Vanisi. Vanisi is sentenced to death and as of 2017 has given up appeals. 1420 Hillside Drive, Reno, Nevada. Built to Spill, "The Plan."

"Poem with Names Carved into It"—Hurricane Irma, 2017.

"Yellow, Rabbits"—It's Picasso (duh): the Don Quixote ink on paper drawing. And the sun isn't yellow at all. It's all black and white. I don't know why I remembered it that way.

"Nocturne"—Juliet Patterson and Rachel Moritz, thank you. Mikhail Bakhtin. Vincent Van Gogh, "Painter on His Way to Work." One rainy afternoon at the Little Falls Golf Course, Little Falls, Minnesota, I mis-used the machine for laminating new member cards in order to laminate a small handful of the pubic hair of my friend Todd Lee, who is not a tennis executive.

Kari Houser, Claire Stobb, Carter Stobb: I'll love you fiercely, exactly as you are, until I'm dead, and after that too if it's possible.

ACKNOWLEDGMENTS

American Poetry Review: "Capitol Street Pulse," "Sam Says Everything,"
        "Album," and "Freedom"
Colorado Review: "Interval"
Diode: "Entropic" and "A Public Service Announcement"
Donga: "The Conclusive Gesture Becomes Visible"
Driftwood: "Dig"
Enizagam: "Speed Wobbles"
Hobart: "The Future," "Time," and "Identity"
Ink Node: "A Message from Your Mode" and "*Wunderkammer*" (*Ink Node*
        editors' features)
Interim: "Capital of Bears"
Jujubes: "Fun," "During a Panic Attack, I Watch a Buddhist Documentary"
Kenyon Review: "What Is Happening"
MiPOesias: "The Dream of Perfect Pants" and "Surface Tension"
North American Review: "Doom"
Passages North: "Meaning"
Poets & Artists: "Of Birth and Panama" and "Dead and Alive"
Sierra Nevada Review: "Contact. It's Heartbreaking"
Science Fiction Poetry Association: "Sorry, I Can't Design Your Futuristic Bug Creature"
Spoon River Poetry Review: "A Moment for Authentic Shine"
Two Bridges Review: "Green Apple Inn" and "Poem with the Virgin Mary"

"A Message from Your Mode" also appeared in *Hybrid*, a portfolio by Thomas
Ferrella and Sara Parrel, with prints appearing in Milwaukee taxis.

"A Moment for Authentic Shine" earned *Spoon River Poetry Review*'s Editor's Prize.

"Fun" is featured in "My Wisconsin," a video presentation by historian Ariel Beaujot.

"Sorry, I Can't Design Your Futuristic Bug Creature" earned first prize in the
Science Fiction Poetry Association open contest.

The title *You Are Still Alive* comes from artworks by Landon Sheely.
See landonsheely.com. I'm grateful for his permission to use it here.

William Stobb is the author of five previous poetry collections, including *Absentia*, the National Poetry Series selection, *Nervous Systems*, and *Artifact Eleven: Desert Fragments*, which reflects on the work of earth artist, Michael Heizer. Stobb's poems have appeared in *American Poetry Review*, *Colorado Review*, *Conduit*, *Denver Quarterly*, *DIAGRAM*, *Interim*, *Jacket*, *Kenyon Review*, *MiPOesias*, and many other journals and zines. Stobb now works as part of the editorial team at *Conduit* and its book publishing division, Conduit Books & Ephemera. He lives near the Mississippi River in Onalaska, Wisconsin, and teaches on the Creative Writing faculty at the University of Wisconsin - La Crosse.